Who on Earth is Dian Fossey?

Defender of the Mountain Gorillas

Jill Menkes Kushner

Enslow Publishers, Inc.
40 Industrial Road
Box 398
Berkeley Heights, NJ 07922
USA

http://www.enslow.com

*To my family of warm, playful primates . . . with much love
and thanks for the pleasure you bring me every day.*

Library of Congress Cataloging-in-Publication Data

Kushner, Jill Menkes.
    Who on earth is Dian Fossey? : defender of the mountain gorillas / Jill Menkes Kushner.
        p. cm. — (Scientists saving the earth)
    Includes bibliographical references and index.
    Summary: "Details Dian Fossey's life, with chapters devoted to her early years, life, work, writings,
and legacy, as well as how children can follow in her footsteps"—Provided by publisher.
    ISBN-13: 978-1-59845-117-7
    ISBN-10: 1-59845-117-0
    1. Fossey, Dian—Juvenile literature. 2. Primatologists—United States—Biography—Juvenile
literature. 3. Gorilla—Rwanda—Juvenile literature. I. Title.
    QL31.F65K87 2009
    599.884092—dc22
    [B]
                                        2008029376

Printed in the United States of America

10 9 8 7 6 5 4 3 2 1

To Our Readers:
We have done our best to make sure all Internet Addresses in this book were active and appropriate
when we went to press. However, the author and the publisher have no control over and assume no
liability for the material available on those Internet sites or on other Web sites they may link to. Any
comments or suggestions can be sent by e-mail to comments@enslow.com or to the address on the
back cover.

♻ Enslow Publishers, Inc., is committed to printing our books on recycled paper. The paper in every
book contains 10% to 30% post-consumer waste (PCW). The cover board on the outside of each book
contains 100% PCW. Our goal is to do our part to help young people and the environment too!

Photo Credits: © Anastasia Poland, p. 60; © Anthony De Lannoy, pp. 74, 83; © Antoine
Sanfuentes/Associated Press, p. 96; © AP/Wide World Photos, p. 58; © Associated Press, p. 35;
© Brenton Kelly/Associated Press, p. 85; © Dian Fossey Gorilla Fund International, p. 8; © Durova,
p. 18 (bottom); © Enslow Publishers, Inc., pp. 11, 38; © Gerry Ellis/Getty Images, pp. 12–13, 15, 18,
26, 32, 46, 98; NASA/JPL, pp. 89, 92; © John Moore/Getty Images, p. 67; © iStockphoto.com/Yves
Grau, pp. 6–7, 24; © Photos.com, p. 64; © Robert M. Campbell/*National Geographic*, pp. 36–37; 49;
© Sarel Kromer, p. 54; © smartneddy, p. 18(top); © Topham/The Image Works, p. 86; U.S. Bureau
of Land Management, p. 22(top).

Cover Photo: Dian Fossey with Pucker. © Robert M. Campbell/*National Geographic*.

Contents

Read about other Scientists
Saving the Earth

Introduction

It was 1963. Dian Fossey had been waiting for years for this moment. She had traveled thousands of miles. She was about to see a mountain gorilla for the very first time.

It was humid, the air thick in the dense forest. Even before she saw the animals, she knew she was in gorilla territory. She inhaled their strong scent as she approached their nesting place. The smell was powerful, a combination of farm odor and something else that seemed almost human and familiar.

Then she heard the gorillas' cries as they greeted one another. Their calls and yells split the air around them, a challenge to the ears.

The tracker carefully cut aside the brush. At last Fossey could see them clearly. There were six of them, all adults. Their slick black faces stared back at the visitors with wonder. What is this species? They look different. But they are not a threat; we know that much. Well, we will entertain them for a while. The huge animals beat their chests with great showiness as if to say, "See us? This is our playtime. Are you impressed by our great size and sounds?" They yawned, limbs outstretched.

Then Fossey heard one of the trackers next to her, speaking to himself. He exclaimed in Swahili: "Kweli nudugu yanga!" (Surely, God, these are my kin!) She found herself overwhelmed. At the same moment, she realized that she had found her life's work. She would learn about the gorillas. She would become part of their world. And she would become closer to these majestic, unique beings than anyone ever had before.

View of the Virunga Volcanoes in Africa, where Dian Fossey studied mountain gorillas.

Digit's World

Of all the gorillas she came to know, Digit became Dian Fossey's favorite. With Digit, she created a bond stronger than life and death. The two formed a relationship between an animal and a human that became an extraordinary example of a friendship between two different species. How did such an amazing relationship happen?

Dian Fossey with Digit

Gentle Creatures

Fossey met Digit in 1967, when he was five years old. He was a blackback—a young male—in Group 4. The gorillas traveled in separate groups, or families. Fossey identified them by number. She gave the gorillas names that suited their personalities or features. She named Digit for his crooked middle finger.

Very early on, Digit was a scamp. He would roll onto the lap of Uncle Bert, the group's silverback leader, who was named for Fossey's favorite uncle. Uncle Bert would tickle Digit with flowers and leaves, and Digit would break into loud sounds of glee.

Fossey would watch the five youngsters as they trailed after Uncle Bert. They galloped from one tree trunk to another. Digit play-wrestled with his sisters while the adults rested. Sometimes, they paraded in front of Fossey and beat their chests, seeking her attention. Fossey was charmed by Digit.

Developing a Relationship

The younger gorillas in Group 4, especially Digit, welcomed Fossey. They treated her almost as one of their own. As their relationship developed, she tickled the infants like a loving grandmother. She and they would groom one another, nap together in the sunlight, and make friendly family noises.

As he became older, three of Digit's half sisters went to other groups. In her book, *Gorillas in the Mist,* Fossey guesses that at this point, the other gorillas in his group became either too old or too young for him to play with. He grew more interested in humans. When researchers came around to observe him, he seemed pleased. If Fossey brought new visitors, he would smell their clothing or touch their hair.

Digit even behaved differently toward men and women. He seemed to understand that they were somehow unlike one another. With men, he would gently hit them or make a playful, fake charge. With women, he behaved more shyly. However, if Fossey appeared alone, he would plop onto his back and wave his legs in the air, inviting her to play. At these times, she would briefly neglect her note taking to enjoy the amazement of playing with a member of another species.

Digit was intrigued by the equipment Fossey brought with her. He liked her notebooks, her gloves, and especially her camera. He examined these items by handling and sniffing them. One day, she brought a mirror, and he sniffed it. Then he looked at his reflection, puzzling over it with a sigh. Next, he reached behind the glass, possibly to find the "other" gorilla. Touching air, he stared again for a while, still puzzled. But he seemed to enjoy trying to figure out what he was looking at.

Tourist Attraction

Six years after she first met Digit, the Rwandan tourism office asked Fossey for a photograph of a gorilla. The country was trying to attract visitors. She gave them a photo of Digit from which they created a poster. It was displayed in Rwanda and in travel agencies around the world. The caption read: "Come and See Me in Rwanda!"[1]

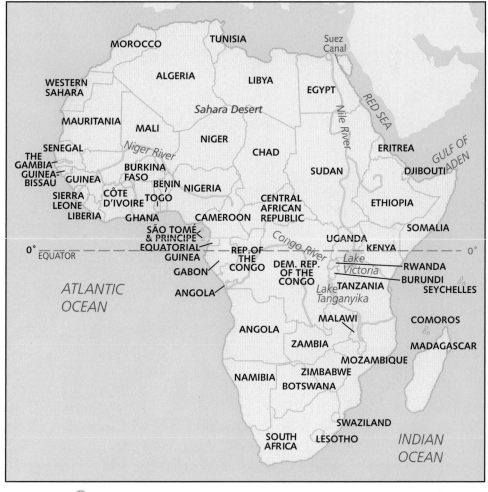

Map of Africa. The country of Rwanda is highlighted in yellow.

A mountain gorilla group. Note the reddish hair of the baby clinging to its mother.

It was odd that Digit was the gorilla chosen for this poster. Just as it appeared, he was growing less interested in humans. He was taking a more adult role in Group 4 as a protector.

Fossey had mixed feelings about exposing the mountain gorillas to the world at large. Digit's group, Group 4, was becoming a strong family unit. Fossey was concerned that an increase in outside interest would threaten the tranquil environment that the gorillas—and she—lived in. But she had no idea how drastically things would change.

The Background for Fossey's Work

Scientists label animals with Latin names in order to be able to talk about them in an organized way. They group them into species and subspecies. In 1758, biologist Carl Linnaeus came up with the label Primates to group humans with gorillas, chimpanzees, and orangutans. The label conveys their high status within the animal world.

Gorillas have long been of interest to humans, partly because of their size and power. In addition, along with the other primates, they are one of the closest of all primates to humans in their structure, behavior, and genetic makeup.

Scientists have identified more than a 95 percent similarity in the genetic makeup of humans

Mountain gorilla families are close-knit groups and may number up to thirty members.

and of gorillas. Therefore, studies of gorillas are vital to a better understanding our own species.

Primates share certain characteristics. They have no tails, and they have five digits on each hand and foot. The first digit on each hand is opposable, meaning that it can turn back against the other fingers. This characteristic allows the hand to use fine motor skills, including the ability to hold objects.

Primates also share the quality of having binocular vision, which is the ability to use two eyes at the same time. Humans tend to take this feature for granted. However, there are strong advantages in having binocular vision, especially for creatures that live in the wild. This characteristic allows an animal to have a wide field of vision. Primates can find small objects, and they can sense depth. These traits are needed for self-protection and obtaining food.

In addition, primates generally have a total of thirty-two teeth. Mountain gorillas, like humans, possess a large brain and provide a long period of care to infants.

Understanding Mountain Gorillas

Gorillas are the largest living primate. Males can weigh from about 340 pounds, with a height of about 5 feet 7 inches. Females can weigh about 185 pounds and are several inches shorter than the males. The mountain gorilla is hairier than other gorillas. Its long, silken black hair covers much of its body, but its face is bare.

Contrary to rumors, gorillas are nonaggressive. They are gentle unless they sense a threat. They spend much of their time eating, an activity that they fully enjoy.

The mountain gorilla was officially classified in 1903. It is scientifically known as *Gorilla gorilla beringei,* named after the hunter and explorer Robert "Oskar" von Beringe. He was a German officer who found mountain gorillas in the Congo. Later work with mountain gorillas continued mostly due to the efforts of Carl Akeley and George Schaller.

Carl Akeley, like von Beringe, was also a hunter. However, after studying the mountain gorillas, he became interested in their preservation. Akeley convinced the Belgian government, which controlled the Kabara region of the Congo, to establish the Albert National Park in 1925. The park was set up to protect the habitat of the mountain gorillas, whose ancestors had lived in the region for four hundred thousand years. After Akeley died, he was buried in the meadow at Kabara.

In 1959, George Schaller led a two-year field study of mountain gorillas in Africa. He and his team logged in more than 450 hours of research in

George Schaller described his first silverback as the "most magnificent animal" he had ever seen. This mountain gorilla sports the characteristic silver-streaked hair of the mature male.

Kabara, a region in Africa that lies at an altitude of 10,200 feet. Schaller saw that the mountain gorillas were far gentler than people had thought. He also saw them as individuals that were unique.

Louis Leakey, a famous archaeologist, also understood the need to study the mountain gorilla. Leakey studied human fossils in remote parts of the world. He established the Leakey Foundation in 1968 to support studies of evolution.

Leakey worried that the mountain gorilla might become extinct. He wanted George Schaller's work to continue. In addition, Leakey hoped that a mountain gorilla project would be as successful as Jane Goodall's work with chimpanzees. Goodall was studying chimps in the region of Lake Tanganyika in central Africa.

Luckily, Leakey and Dian Fossey met, and her work became scientific history. As things turned out, Fossey's work was the start of more than thirty years of continuous observation. In fact, some of the descendants of the gorillas she observed are still being studied today.

Dian Fossey's Early Life and the Beginning of Her Dream

Despite the fame Dian Fossey came to have in her adult life, little is known about her early life. She was born on January 16, 1932, in California. She had a difficult childhood. Her relationship with her parents was a challenge for both her and them. Her father had financial problems, and her parents divorced when she was three years old. She lived with her mother, Kitty, and her stepfather, but they were not close.

Fossey continued to keep in contact with her father, George, through letters and photographs. She also kept his last name as her own. Unfortunately, when Fossey was an adult, her father committed suicide.

Ambitions Take Root

It is clear that Dian Fossey had an early, strong love for all animals. One of her favorite jobs was when she spent a summer in Montana taking care of horses. Her first desire was to be a veterinarian. However, she had trouble with some of the more difficult subjects.

Fossey then studied to become an occupational therapist. She wanted to help people in need. She decided to work with children. She took a job at a children's hospital in Louisville, Kentucky, and worked there for eleven years.

Fossey was good at her work. Many of the children suffered from polio. She approached them in a very quiet way. She did not push them to communicate with her. Instead, she allowed them to become closer to her when they were ready.

In addition, she was able to foster her love of animals by living in a cottage on an old farm. There were possums, cattle, cats, and farm dogs to care for or just to enjoy. She nurtured them as she developed her interest in caring for living things.

Louis Leakey examining skulls from Olduvai Gorge, Africa.

A cast made from the original skull discovered by Mary Leakey, Olduvai Gorge, Tanzania 1959. Mary Leakey found the skull of a humanlike creature at Olduvai Gorge, Tanzania. This creature, called *Australopithecus boisei*, lived about 1,750,000 years ago. This discovery was one of the first indications that humanlike beings lived in prehistoric eastern Africa.

A Taste of Africa

In 1960, after hearing about a friend's travels to Africa and seeing photographs of its scenery and animals, Fossey was determined to visit there. She decided to take out an eight-thousand-dollar bank loan—an enormous amount of money at the time. She planned a trip that would last seven weeks. In preparation, she studied Swahili and purchased books, clothing, and insect repellent.

Her friends and relatives thought she was crazy to take on such a debt for a trip. Her loan interest rate was extremely high. Even her beloved Uncle Bert and Aunt Flossie, who had helped her financially when she was in school, wanted her to call off the trip. However, firm in her desire, Fossey went to Africa in September 1963. Accompanied by a guide, she saw baboons, buffaloes, lions, zebras, impalas, and rhinoceroses. She fell in love with the country, hoping soon to see the mountain gorillas she had heard about.

Meeting Dr. Leakey

Fossey and her guide traveled to Olduvai Gorge in Tanzania. Fossey wanted to meet Louis Leakey. He and his wife, Mary, were there studying fossils. Leakey's work had been going on since the 1930s. He had proved that humankind had been around for a long time—far longer than others had suspected.

By the time Fossey met Leakey in the 1960s, he was world famous. However, she took a chance on finding him in the hopes that he would speak with her. She learned about Jane Goodall's work with chimpanzees from Leakey. In addition to taking photographs of his study area, she expressed her passionate desire to learn more about mountain gorillas. Then, she and her guide headed into Uganda to the Congo to see the gorillas.

First Encounter

First, Fossey stopped at the Traveller's Rest hotel, near the Uganda-Congo-Rwanda border. Scientists and researchers often stopped there to exchange the latest news about gorillas. From the hotel, she could hike to the Virunga volcanoes, where the mountain gorillas lived.

There Fossey learned that noted wildlife photographers Joan and Alan Root had a camp nearby. Although

Virunga Volcanoes

Dian Fossey's first glimpse of mountain gorillas through the dense foliage of the African forest led her to vow to return.

they were absorbed in their work, they helped her find mountain gorillas.

According to Fossey's notes, the mountain gorillas were impressive and large. But she did not find them threatening. Their black slick faces seemed to be measuring the humans and their possible danger. As Alan Root filmed the gorillas, they showed curiosity about the observers. The gorillas then seemed to playact for their visitors. They gave a show of yawning and chest beating.

After her trip, Fossey returned to Kentucky. She went back to work, mainly to pay off her loan. But her heart was no longer there. It had traveled halfway around the world.

Meeting Dr. Leakey—Again

Luckily for Fossey, Louis Leakey happened to be lecturing in Kentucky in 1966. Fossey went to see him, and he remembered having met her. He was impressed by articles she had written on gorillas. Leakey again discussed Jane Goodall's work, for which he had raised funding. Goodall had been studying chimpanzees in Tanzania for six years by this time. He expressed his belief that women made excellent field researchers. He felt that their patience was of great value.

Much to Fossey's surprise and delight, Leakey invited her to become the "gorilla girl."[1] She would lead a long-term mountain gorilla study in a remote location near the Virunga volcanoes in Africa. Fossey expressed concern about her inexperience and her limited science background. Leakey dismissed her lack of self-confidence. He told Fossey that he preferred someone who was not overtrained. He wanted a person who did not have rigid ideas. They also discussed George Schaller's studies of mountain gorillas. Fossey made the commitment to continue the work Schaller had started.

Leakey convinced The Wilkie Brothers' Foundation—which had funded Goodall's work— and the National Geographic Society to finance the project. Fossey packed her clothes, cameras, and hundreds of rolls of film. She left the United States in December 1966 with few plans to return.

Work Begins

At first, Fossey had only her determination to keep her going. In addition to having no experience or training in living in the wilderness, she was not in good health. She had many physical problems. On arriving in Africa, she actually had pneumonia. This disease makes it very difficult to breathe at high altitudes, such as those in the forest where she would conduct her research. But nothing would stop her.

Fossey gained help from Joan and Alan Root. They were the nature photographers who knew her from her earlier visit to Africa. They were concerned about Fossey. She planned to travel seven hundred miles from Nairobi to the Congo, communicate with authorities there, and set up camp—all completely on her own.

The Roots helped her buy supplies and set up camp. Leakey then helped Fossey choose a vehicle that could handle the rough land. It was a Land Rover, which she named "Lily." Fossey then went to see Jane Goodall and her husband at the Gombe research station. There she learned how to run a camp. Goodall taught Fossey how to organize her living space and the data she planned to collect.

Hearing of Fossey's plans, Louis Leakey's wife Mary commented that Fossey was going to "out-Schaller Schaller."[2] It was an overwhelming thought to the inexperienced newcomer. However, Fossey knew that she wanted to approach the study differently from Schaller. He had not observed the mountain gorillas at close range. She wanted to learn about their social relationships. More importantly, she wanted to interact with them.

Adventures in Africa

In January 1967, Fossey set up camp in the Congo. She hired local men to help her carry her equipment and supplies four thousand feet up to Kabara Meadow. It was a difficult five-hour climb into high altitudes. The porters who accompanied her had to lug camp supplies such as food and equipment.

The living conditions were extremely rough in that first camp. At first Fossey lived in a seven-by-ten-foot canvas tent. It served many purposes. The tent was her bedroom, office, and a place to bathe. She also hung her clothes there to dry, although in the constant mist of the rain forest, everything, including clothes, stayed damp.

Once each month, she drove two hours to get supplies and canned food.

Alan Root took Fossey on her first outing teaching her how to follow gorilla tracks. Her choice of Kabara seemed to be a promising one. The very next day she heard gorilla noises about a half mile from camp.

Animal Sights and Sounds

Fossey soon saw gorillas. Then she started thinking about how best to approach them. Her first few days in the forest taught her some amusing lessons.

At first, Fossey used a park guard as her temporary guide. He was clearly not a tracking expert. She spent much of her third day observing what she thought was a sunbathing gorilla. Finally, she approached the animal, only to discover that it was a giant hog! Shortly after this experience, a skilled guide named Sanwekwe—who had assisted George Schaller—came to help her as a tracker.

On her fourth night at the Kabara campsite, Fossey was awakened abruptly by three elephants. They were scratching themselves against her tent poles. After this experience, she became used to almost daily encounters with a variety of animal wanderers. There were elephants, buffalo, tree hyrax, antelope, and hogs. In addition, Fossey had adopted several pets she kept in camp, including

Mountain gorillas have longer faces and longer and darker hair than lowland gorillas.

a monkey (Kima), a dog (Cindy), two chickens (Lucy and Dezi), and a rooster and chicken couple (Walter and Wilma).

Part of Fossey's responsibility was to record data. She made it part of her daily routine to type up notes based on her observations. She noted all gorilla contacts. Between her fieldwork, recording gorilla sounds, note taking, and the activities needed to maintain the camp, she was kept very busy.

Approaching With Caution

A few days later, Fossey encountered a family of nine gorillas. She named them Group 1. From reading George Schaller's book *The Year of the Gorilla*, Fossey knew that she should remain visible to the gorillas but not appear suddenly. Soon she discovered that they had an intense sense of curiosity. They wanted to know more about this stranger in their midst.

At first, before the gorillas became used to Fossey's presence, they reacted with screams when she approached. Then she realized that imitating their vocalizations would be less frightening to them. When she signaled her approach by mimicking their belching sounds, they no longer saw her as a threat. She also copied their gestures. She pretended to groom herself. She nibbled on celery stalks, and she crouched. Her imitations seemed to please them. However, she learned to avoid copying their chest beating. For gorillas, chest beating communicates alarm or excitement.

Occasionally, Fossey's approach was misinterpreted. Then she had to endure the horrifying charge of a group. But she understood the basic gentle nature of the gorilla. She knew what to do. Instead of fleeing and inviting a chase, she would slowly fall to the ground, staying quiet until they left her alone.

Some natives were convinced that Fossey possessed a special kind of magic, or *sumu*, which protected her from the gorillas' anger.[1] Her experience, however, taught her that gorillas would charge only when they felt threatened, either by humans or other animals, including other gorillas. They attacked only to defend their families.

Building Trust

Fossey started to take out her camera as the gorillas' trust and curiosity increased. During her second month at Kabara, she was able to take a photo of sixteen gorillas. According to Fossey, it appeared as though they were posing for the photographer!

During this experience, as with almost every one of her gorilla encounters, Fossey learned something new. She was having trouble climbing a slippery tree to take the photograph. Finally, she

Dian Fossey is barely noticed as she stands in the midst of a gorilla group.

made it up to the top, with help from Sanwekwe, her tracker. By then, she assumed that all her frustration noises would have scared away the gorillas. But they stayed. In fact, the entire group was staring at her.

As Fossey noted in her book, "That day's observation was a perfect example of how the gorillas' sense of curiosity could be utilized toward their habituation."[2] Because they wanted to learn more about the person who was having problems

Dian Fossey with Pucker.

climbing a tree, they overcame their natural shyness and came into her full view.

Again and again in her studies, Fossey was able to take advantage of the mountain gorillas' inquisitive nature to make them become used to her presence. She worked tirelessly on becoming almost invisible. As the gorillas grew more comfortable, they began to behave more naturally. As a result, Fossey managed to gain rare views of their behavior, activities, and relationships.

The Census Taker

When Fossey first arrived in Africa in the late 1960s, the mountain gorilla population totaled more than two hundred individuals. Fossey's experience at Kabara showed her that three of the groups she was studying matched groups that George Schaller had studied earlier.[3] She determined that there had been a loss of several gorillas during the 1960s.

In addition, she learned that since Schaller's study, the size of the Parc des Volcans (Volcanoes National Park) had been reduced by four thousand acres. This change in the park's size most likely contributed to the decrease in the gorilla population. Fossey realized that an important part of her work would include constantly taking a count to see how many gorillas were alive.

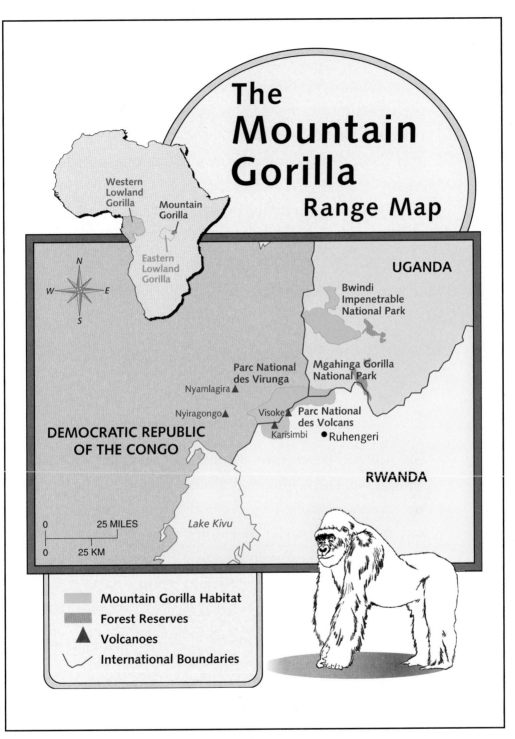

The Mountain Gorilla
Range Map

Western Lowland Gorilla

Mountain Gorilla

Eastern Lowland Gorilla

N
W   E
S

UGANDA

Bwindi Impenetrable National Park

Parc National des Virunga

Mgahinga Gorilla National Park

Nyamlagira ▲

Nyiragongo▲

Visoke▲ Parc National des Volcans

DEMOCRATIC REPUBLIC OF THE CONGO

Karisimbi ▲ ● Ruhengeri

RWANDA

0   25 MILES

0   25 KM

Lake Kivu

Mountain Gorilla Habitat
Forest Reserves
▲ Volcanoes
International Boundaries

Fossey's studies of the mountain gorilla took place along the borders of three countries: Congo, Rwanda, and Uganda.

Evenings in Kabara

Night after night, Fossey's oil lamp would burn as she typed up her field notes, recording the day's research. She studied old bones and skulls, poring over them to add to her growing store of knowledge.

The camp community also enjoyed periods of relaxation, especially during Christmas time. Fossey gave gifts to the staff and their families. The group ate, danced, and sang together, in whatever languages they knew—Kinyarwnada, French, or English. The natives composed drumming songs and dances that became part of an annual gathering.

Rebellion Erupts

The Congo (now the Democratic Republic of Congo) has had a long and difficult history. Early on, it was controlled by the country of Portugal and later came under Belgium's rule. In 1960, the people of the Congo declared their independence. Afterward, many different groups fought for power.

In the summer of 1967, rebellion broke out, ending Fossey's studies at Kabara. The park director sent armed guards to escort her off the mountain. Foreigners were in danger. Because she was living deep in the forest, she had not been aware of outside events. She was very frustrated at having to leave her camp. By then she had identified three different gorilla groups. But she had no choice.

Fossey went to the Traveller's Rest hotel in Uganda, where she had stayed before. Although it was difficult to leave Kabara, within several months she set up camp in Rwanda. Rwanda was also in the middle of a political struggle for independence. However, the unrest had little immediate impact on Fossey's work.

Starting Over in Rwanda

Fossey's close friends, Alyette DeMunck and Rosamond Carr, had lived in the region for years and knew it well. With their help, Fossey tried to find new mountain gorilla territory. Carr told Fossey she would not find gorillas on the Rwandan side of the mountains. Fossey thought differently.

After climbing up Mount Karisimbi—more than fourteen thousand feet high—Fossey noticed a saddle region that lay between Karisimbi and Mount Visoke. She knew the slopes would attract gorillas and set up camp there on September 24, 1967. Her camp sat at an altitude of ten thousand feet in the Parc National des Volcans. Fossey combined the names of the two mountains—Karisimbi to the south and Visoke to the north—to create the name of her camp. She called it Karisoke Research Centre (the spelling was later changed to *Center*).

After the forced interruption of nineteen weeks, she was able to continue her fieldwork.

Working Again

The Virunga mountain range is made up of two active and six dormant volcanoes. Fossey located the gorillas on the dormant volcanoes. The weather was often a challenge. The mornings were very cold, and it often rained for hours or days.

Fossey improved her tracking skills in the Virungas. She learned to follow the gorillas' signals. She would look for bent branches, scratched bark, knuckle prints, and clumps of gorilla droppings.

At Kabara, Fossey had studied three groups, totaling about fifty individual gorillas. In Fossey's first year at Karisoke, she identified more groups. Four groups—Groups 4, 5, 8, and 9—were the main focus of her attention.

She gave the gorillas names. No-nose was the first, followed by others—Solomon, Hugger, Popcorn, Tagalong—including Peanuts, Digit, and the infants Coco and Pucker, the four gorillas with whom she developed special relationships.

Fossey discovered the close family ties of the mountain gorillas. Each group had a structure. The silverbacks were the dominant members. They took care of the rest of the group. Each family nurtured and protected all of its members.

Fieldwork Becomes Scholarship

Gorillas descended from an ancestor that lived in the trees. Over time, they came to live on the ground and have become the most earthbound of all the apes. Groups usually range in number between 5 and 10.

As Fossey discovered during her observations, gorillas are active during the daytime and sleep at night, although they also nap during the day. About 40 percent of their day is spent resting. The remainder of their day is equally divided between feeding and traveling. Sometimes they travel and eat at the same time.[1] Mountain gorillas normally walk and run on their knuckles. When they are chest beating, they stand upright and walk or run for a short while in this position.

Because they travel to find food, mountain gorillas build their nighttime nests in a different place each night. Their nests are soft and leafy oval shapes, usually on the ground. Sometimes they create nests in tree trunks. Food sources such as decayed bark and roots are located there. If the animals suspect that poachers are nearby, they choose nesting spots that have a good view of the surrounding area.

By the time a male reaches full maturity at about fifteen years, the hair on his back has become short and turned silver white. This characteristic is the reason that fully adult males are called silverbacks. Wild gorillas who make it past infancy may live for twenty-five to thirty years but not much more.

Males compete over females, so they can have several opportunities in their group to mate. Unlike other primates, the bond between each female and the male leader keeps the group together. (In other primate groups, bonding is stronger among female group members.) There are also sometimes disputes within a group when food is limited. In this case, the male group leader typically feeds first. Then he allows the rest of the group to feed and fight over whatever is left.

Sounds

Throughout the day, gorillas typically make quiet, belching-type noises to signal a variety of activities, including eating, moving, or even resting. As one gorilla vocalizes, others answer. Fossey learned that all of their sounds had particular meanings, and she knew which ones to imitate. One of her techniques was to make quiet "contentment" noises.[2] This sound was one of their recognized forms of communication. Fossey found that their level of contentment was highest on warm days filled with sunlight. They communicated happy noises back and forth.

Sometimes after resting in the middle of the day, gorillas will grunt at one another. These grunts indicate that they are finished resting and are about to move on. They make additional sounds for other purposes. A cough-type sound signals minor aggression. A bark serves as an alarm call. In addition, an infant will whimper if it is lost or scream to show fear.

Silverbacks use a kind of piglike grunting noise to settle group disputes or to indicate displeasure. Females make this noise to show annoyance about food disagreements or to wean their infants. Young gorillas will grunt to convey that another gorilla is playing too roughly with them. The meaning is never in doubt. It is a warning to other gorillas to stop whatever they are doing.

Nesting gorillas

Food

Gorillas are vegetarians, eating a wide variety of plants. They enjoy bamboo, giant celery, and other vines, leaves, stems, roots, and grasses. In the area where Dian Fossey did her research, the gorillas ate ferns that grew on *Hagenia* trees, plants on the *Hypericum* tree, and buds from the *Vernonia* tree.

Fossey found that from the lowlands to the higher regions, the gorillas fed upon more than fifty species of plants. They ate a lot of the *Galium* vine, which grows in many altitude levels of the forest. The vine also grows both on the ground and in treetops.[3] Mountain gorillas also eat fungi, snails, grubs, and, very rarely, fruit.

The fact that they do not eat much fruit contributes to the stability of the mountain gorilla groups. Because vegetation is easy to find, the group can stay together. If mountain gorillas had to forage individually to find fruit—which is only available during certain seasons—they would naturally separate from one another.

Noses

Fossey continued to behave like the gorillas so they would ignore her. She even pretended to pick bugs out of her hair!

Fossey also sketched the nose prints of the gorillas. Every gorilla's nose print is defined by the indentations above its nostrils and the shape of its nose. Like human fingerprints, nose prints are unique. Fossey and her staff would use binoculars to help them draw the sketches. Later, they compared the markings to photographs to identify individual gorillas.

Peanuts

A little less than a year after she had set up camp at Karisoke, Fossey "crossed an intangible barrier" between herself and the gorillas.[4] First, a quiet but memorable event happened. Peanuts, the youngest male in Group 8, stared directly at Fossey during a pause in his feeding. She returned his glance. There was a moment of understanding and acceptance between them.

Then, two years later in 1970, Peanuts came over to Fossey one day during his feeding time. She had been copying the gorillas' in their eating behavior, as she often did. Peanuts sat beside her. Again imitating gorilla behavior, she scratched her head. He then scratched his head. Next, she lay down in the leaves with her hand extended. Peanuts considered the familiar-looking object and touched his fingers to hers. He then stood, excitedly beat his chest, and returned to his group.

This brief moment became history. Photographer and fellow researcher Robert Campbell captured the event for the international nature

Peanuts and Fossey interacting. In early years among the gorillas Fossey won their tolerance, but in early 1970 she at last achieved overt acceptance.

magazine, *National Geographic*. The world would see the first recorded contact between a human and a mountain gorilla.

Learning About Groups 8 and 9

Group 8 had no infants in the group. As a result, Fossey noticed, there was no need for strongly protective behavior. However, the group members were often affectionate with one another. They were a tight family unit. The leader, Rafiki, was mature and capable. Fossey found that the group habituated itself to her presence very quickly.

Fossey had first located Group 9 in 1968. However, by 1971, Fossey and her staff had increasing difficulty locating Group 9. She knew that the leader, Geronimo, had disappeared and most likely died. This experience also eventually occurred with Group 8.

Fossey learned this characteristic was common in mountain gorilla families. When the silverback leader dies, if there is no available maturing male leader to take over the group, the group falls apart. Then its members separate and look for new groups to belong to.

Group Dynamics

One of the things that Fossey learned and relearned was that the gorillas displayed different personality features, based on their roles. Most groups generally included a dominant, older silverback male, at least two females with whom the silverback could mate, a younger male, and some infants. There were occasional variations in this makeup. One group consisted of only adults. Another included a younger male as the only male. However, the groups always seemed to strive for a basic balance that consisted of an older silverback and females for mating.

There was a constant interplay between different groups to reestablish this balance when group members died due to natural causes or outside interference. Movement to different groups was very common, but it was not always conducted peacefully.

Of the five groups she studied at Karisoke, Fossey felt she learned much about family relationships from Group 5. "[They] have taught me how the strong bonds of kinship contribute towards the cohesiveness of a gorilla family unit over time."[5]

However, the behavior of all gorillas was not predictable. Certain males were better leaders, and certain females were better nurturers.

Males

For example, Beethoven, the leader of Group 5, was much more mature than Uncle Bert, the leader of Group 4. Beethoven usually treated Uncle Bert with patience. However, eventually Uncle Bert confronted Beethoven in a dispute over Bravado. Bravado, a female, had once been part of Group 4 and then transferred to Group 5.

First, Uncle Bert beat his chest. Then Beethoven stood and beat his chest in response, signaling his readiness to protect his group. Finally, the two gorillas went back to their own groups.

Then, unpredictably, Bravado took some of the other younger members of Group 5 over to play with Group 4's younger members. Perhaps she remembered her old group and the playfulness of its youngsters. In any case, Beethoven rushed into Group 4's area and grabbed her, even though he was surrounded. He grunted at her and the other Group 5 deserters to come with him as he started to walk away.

Uncle Bert beat his chest several times and made a series of loud noises. Beethoven turned back. But then he led his group away. The dispute ended, with both leaders returning to their own groups.

What Fossey found striking was that the interaction was a perfect example of how far the gorillas would go to avoid physical confrontation. Although they sometimes inflicted wounds on one another, the injuries were not generally fatal. The leaders of each group saw their responsibility to the group as their most important role. They did not engage in confrontation for its own sake.

Females

Females also displayed differences. They varied greatly in their mothering skills. Effie, of Group 5, had a kind, relaxed attitude toward her children. On the other hand, Marchessa, also of Group 5, was impatient with her male offspring, Ziv.

Old Goat of Group 4 was a "model" mother. Flossie, in the same group, gave far less attention to the grooming and care of her infants. There was also evidence of "aunt behavior" in Maisie of Group 4.[6] She would sometimes care for Flossie's offspring. Fossey assumed that aunt behavior was practice for motherhood.

Certain females had more power than others in the group. Sometimes females would compete for the honor of grooming the silverback. In addition, there was an understood ranking system. For instance, the female named Macho had the least status in Group 4 because she had transferred from another group. Her fear of the other group members showed in her watchful eyes.

Parents had to deal with their children's rowdy behavior. In such cases, the child would usually take an apologetic pose. For instance, Samson, a child in Group 8, bent his arms and lowered his gaze if Rafiki showed disapproval.

Female gorilla with infant at Volcans National Park.

Offspring also showed personality differences. Many were curious, some were restless, and some did not want to separate from their mothers.

Puck, a Group 5 youngster, always wanted to examine Fossey's knapsack. Puck tried Fossey's binoculars, looking through them and even putting his fingers behind the glass. Occasionally, Fossey would have to find an item that he had carried away.

The more Fossey observed, the more she became aware of the behavior of specific gorillas. In 1972, during her contact with Group 4, Fossey tried showing the gorillas a mirror. Some of them stared into it, fascinated. Others—notably Uncle Bert—watched for a short time and then walked away.

Fossey avoided too much contact between the gorillas and mechanical objects, as she was trying to focus on their natural behavior and relationships. However, there was a positive aspect to having them play with nonnatural things. She could observe them at very close range, because they tended to ignore her.

Changes at Karisoke

By 1967, Fossey had gathered 485 hours of observation more than George Schaller. However, she felt that she had not begun to accomplish her goals. She felt that she needed to continue to study the gorillas and to measure their population.

Fossey was asked to write articles for *National Geographic* about her experience. The magazine had been partly responsible for funding her trip. In 1968, Robert Campbell's photos, along with Fossey's articles, gained more publicity for her work. In addition, her friend Alan Root produced a television documentary about her work for

National Geographic that was shown around the world.

People in the outside world were learning about Fossey's discoveries. Her everyday work continued, and she allowed herself no rest. Her only luxury was that she moved from her tent to a homemade cabin.

Expertise Develops

Sanwekwe, an excellent gorilla tracker, taught Fossey much of what she came to know of tracking. With his help and considerable patience, she eventually identified three gorilla groups in her area of study along the slopes of Mt. Mikeno. Fossey in turn taught local people and students to track. The local people quickly took to tracking, although they had to learn the geography of the Virungas.

According to Fossey, following the gorillas was not difficult. In addition to what she already knew, she learned that group members do not travel directly behind one another. Individuals often take steps off the main path to feed. She learned to follow the main trail and taught others to do the same.

In addition, Fossey found that crawling along the trail helped her locate gorillas. On the ground, she could smell the exceptionally strong odor that

Dian Fossey and one of the gorillas she studied at Karisoke. Fossey became a celebrity in 1970 when her photograph, with her gorillas, graced the cover of *National Geographic* magazine. This photograph was taken nine months later.

was produced by the palms and soles of gorillas on the earth and low-lying plants.

Travel Beckons

Fossey was known as *Nyiramachabelli* by the local people, meaning "the old lady who lives in the forest without a man."[1] She would have been happy to remain at Karisoke with her gorillas. But the outside world began to call to her in the late 1960s.

There were several reasons that she needed to travel. First, she thought she should earn a doctorate. She felt that although she had done a lot of fieldwork, she needed a formal education. She was invited to study at Cambridge University in Cambridge, England.

In addition, Louis Leakey and others expressed concerns about Fossey's health. When she had first visited Africa in the 1960s, she was not well. Years spent living in the forest and mountain climate had not improved her health. Finally, she wanted to visit her parents and friends in the United States. Although Fossey was not close to her mother and stepfather, she still felt she should visit them.

Between 1971 and 1976, Fossey traveled between Karisoke, the United States, and Cambridge. She was becoming an internationally known figure. She spoke to audiences and showed slides of the gorillas. People were impressed by

⬆ *Replica of Dian Fossey's Karisoke research center.*

her firsthand knowledge as well as her obvious passion for the animals. By 1972, Fossey had counted almost one hundred gorillas in her study area.

The Scientist

The camp at Karisoke continued to expand, with more tents and cabins being built. Some were close to Fossey's cabin. Others were closer to the gorillas' ranging areas so the staff did not have to always go back to camp.

Fossey also added people to her team. One student researcher was Kelly Stewart, the daughter of the famous actor Jimmy Stewart. Despite her background, Kelly was a serious researcher who worked hard. She later went on to write books and articles about her experiences.

In May 1976, Fossey received her doctorate in zoology, based on her study of the mountain gorillas of the Virungas. She became known as one of Leakey's "three primate ladies."[2] She lectured in California with Jane Goodall and Biruté Galdikas, who was studying orangutans in Borneo. By then, unfortunately, Leakey was not alive to see their success. He had died in 1972 after his second heart attack.

As a now-accepted scientist, Fossey had more expectations placed on her. When she returned to camp full-time in 1976, she worked constantly. In addition to tracking, she was responsible for typing up her notes and publishing articles. She had also made a commitment to write a book.

An Ever-Growing Attachment

The longer Fossey worked in Africa, the more she grew attached to the region, the gorillas, and their meaning to her. For example, she observed Group 4 through three deaths, three births, and the leave-taking of three females. As a result, she became more isolated from the outside world.

Fossey's detailed records were invaluable. However, she knew that a study of many generations was needed to fully understand the gorillas' social relationships. She believed in Karisoke's importance as a long-term center for field research.

Commitment

Fossey depended on many Africans to support her work. Some of them worked tirelessly as porters, carrying supplies up and down the mountain. Others prepared special foods and nesting environments for sick animals. Still others functioned as trackers. They knew the land well and could help researchers locate regions where gorillas were likely to roam. Without the help of these people, Fossey would not have been able to accomplish her goals of researching and protecting the mountain gorillas. It is clear that their efforts mirrored her own.

Ironically, Fossey even received occasional help from some of the cattle ranchers who allowed their cattle to graze in the gorillas' habitat. They assisted her in foiling the efforts of poachers through their knowledge of the countryside.

Tourism Invades

When in 1971, the Rwanda tourist office asked for a photograph of Digit, Fossey was unprepared for worldwide publicity. She wanted to be able to fully study the four groups of gorillas. She also wanted to live in isolation with her staff and her small group of camp animals.

However, as her work became better known, tourists, photographers, and journalists would show up uninvited. Incredibly, some would show up at her door, demanding to see the gorillas. They treated her as though she was a tour guide. Others would ask her staff to do chores for them. Fossey, her students, and the other members of her staff found ways to avoid these unwelcome interruptions. They would lead people on a false trail, or she would hide in her cabin until they left.

Group 5 tended to roam in the eastern portion of Karisoke, so it was most affected by the presence of tourists. But it was not tourism that presented the greatest threat. Other groups in more removed areas—4, 8, 9, and the newly discovered "Nunkie's group"—had to protect themselves against dangerous poachers.[3] Fossey had first observed Nunkie in 1972, traveling alone in the hills and occasionally interacting with members of Groups 4 and 5.

The Scientist Becomes the Protector

Although the Parc des Volcans (Volcanoes National Park) of Rwanda was supposed to be a protected area, many people paid no attention to its status

For people living off the land in rural Africa, life is difficult. Learning to share that land with mountain gorillas and other wildlife has not always been easy.

as a refuge for gorillas. When Fossey first arrived there in 1967, the Parc des Volcans was not staffed or set up to be a refuge. There were very few guards. Little attention was paid to people who wandered through the park.

Native Farmers

There were several forces that Fossey had to deal with as she tried to protect the gorillas' habitat, their way of life, and her ability to study them. First, Watutsi natives were trying to earn a living as cattle farmers, as their families had done for centuries. The farmers would often lead their cattle through the forest. They trampled the gorillas' food source and forced them higher up into the mountains, where there was little food.

It was clear that the mountain gorillas' survival depended upon being able to live at a lower elevation. Although the presence of cattle was difficult to deal with, at least Fossey could understand that the cattle herders were continuing a tradition that went back for generations. There were also natives trying to cultivate pyrethrum, a plant related to the chrysanthemum and used to make insecticide. Increasing plots of land were dedicated to its growth, further encroaching on gorilla territory.

6

Conflict

The worst trespassers were the poachers. The word *poacher* comes from a French word that means "pocket." It suggests the action of putting something into a bag.[1] There were two different types of poachers. There were the local Batwas, who hunted hyrax and antelope in the region, as they had done for hundreds of years. They used arrows, spears, and traps. Unfortunately, their traps also severely wounded or killed gorillas.

In addition, some of the natives, along with officials who were corrupt, sought gorillas for private foreign collectors or zoos. The poachers

Gorilla caregiver Andre Bauma holds four-month-old lowland gorilla Tumaini at the Dian Fossey Gorilla Center in Goma, in the eastern Democratic Republic of Congo. Tumaini, which means "hope" in the Kiswahill language, was rescued from poachers two months ago and arrived at the center in poor health. She and other gorillas are cared for by gorilla specialists trying to preserve the dwindling population of the great apes in Congo usually wanted baby gorillas. But in order to get the babies, they would often kill the other family members. Also, adult gorillas—especially silverbacks—were believed by some natives to have special magic. Therefore, some of them were killed to sell their skulls and hands as trophies. Poachers were responsible for two-thirds of gorilla deaths at the time Fossey published *Gorillas in the Mist* in 1983.

The poachers would camp out in *ikiboogas*— makeshift shelters in the bases of *Hagenia* trees—when they were hunting. Their fires, extra traps, and food enabled Fossey to find their camp locations. She and her staff destroyed campsites, cut down traps, and threw out materials used to make snares.

The traps varied. They might be made of wire with bamboo limbs that served as springs. They might be pits that went as deep as twelve feet. Or, they might be nooses located in the dense brush. When she could, Fossey rescued trapped animals and healed them at her campsite.

Fossey was also given money from the Leakey Foundation to equip camp guards. In addition to removing traps, the guards patrolled and pro-tected the park's boundaries. The efforts of Fossey and her staff produced slow but steady progress. By 1971, the cattle and poachers had been cleared from the area enough for gorillas to return from

the crowded, less vegetated mountains to which
they had retreated for safety.

Culture Clash

The problems that plagued Fossey could, in part,
be understood as a conflict between two different
ways of life. She, along with other wildlife scientists, supported protecting the gorillas' habitat.
Unfortunately, her goals came into conflict with
the economic needs of local people, whether they
were farmers, hunters, or poachers.

This clash was never resolved. It was an almost
predictable result of the entrance of outsiders—
even devoted researchers—into a country that had
been accustomed to certain practices.

A Cold Reality

In 1968, the conservator (director) of the Parc
des Volcans asked Fossey to help him capture an
infant gorilla to export to the Cologne Zoo in Ger-
many. In exchange for the gorilla, the Germans
had offered to donate a Land Rover and money to
the Parc des Volcans for conservation efforts. Fossey was shocked. She stressed the inhumaneness
of the idea. She also explained how strong gorilla
family ties were, and that in order to capture an
infant, adult gorillas would have to be killed.

At the time, she did not realize that many
native officials considered gorillas to be products,

not animals that needed protection. Even park officials were insensitive to the needs of the wildlife in their care. They were often willing to ignore their responsibilities if they could gain personal or political benefit.

In early 1969, Fossey learned that two baby gorillas had been captured, with the knowledge of park authorities. They were scheduled to be sent to the Cologne Zoo. They had been badly treated by their captors and were in poor health.

Coco

The first infant was brought to her to be treated. It was dehydrated and undernourished. Fossey named the infant Coco and took her to the Karisoke camp. Fossey reintroduced Coco to the once familiar forest environment. She comforted Coco with reassuring sounds and fed her vines and other healthful food.

Fossey also turned the second room of her own cabin into Coco's room. It became a mini-forest. Fossey covered the floor with feeding and nesting materials and arranged branches so Coco could climb when she wished.

Her first evening in the cabin, the sick infant climbed onto Fossey's lap. Then, looking out a window toward the mountains, Coco cried, producing tears—an astonishing sight to Fossey that she never again observed.

Pucker

As Coco became healthier, another infant was delivered into Fossey's care. This baby was also destined for the zoo. Fossey named her Pucker, due to the baby's sad expression. Pucker suffered from wounds on her head, hands, and feet. The two infants got acquainted, competed for food, and slept together during Pucker's early days in the camp. Both animals also played with Fossey's dog, Cindy.

These two infant gorillas were unique in that they lived mostly in and around the environment created for them by Fossey. Though it copied the forest environment, it was human-made. They became extremely used to Fossey's presence, even tickling and wrestling with her. However, she was careful not to overdo these actions, keeping her role as observer, rather than participant, most in her mind.

A Sad Good-bye

Fossey's original plan had been to heal the two gorillas. She would then release them into the wild with Group 8. Each time the conservator of the park asked her for the gorillas, she said they were too ill to travel. Finally he said that if she did not return the animals, he would simply send poachers to capture two other infants.

Fossey had to return Coco and Pucker. She had no choice, but, as she wrote: "I felt like a traitor."[2] They were sent to the zoo, and Fossey became very depressed. She later learned that they lived only nine years in captivity (compared to the average life span of a gorilla, which can be more than thirty years), dying in 1978 within one month of each other.

Digit Grows Up

By 1972, Digit seemed to be taking on some of the protective aspects of a more adult male. Usually, Fossey would find him at the border of the group, acting as a guard. Indeed, he seemed to have grown away from her.

However, he definitely remembered the affectionate relationship between them that dated back to his childhood. One rainy day, as she observed him, he came over and put his arm around her. Then he patted her head and sat down by her side. Later, she would treasure this memory.

During 1977, Fossey, along with the rest of the camp staff, increased their antipoaching activity. They also increased their contact with Group 4, Digit's group. The gorillas in that group had moved farther away from the safety of Mount Visoke's slopes.

In early December of 1977, Fossey had what would be her final contact with Digit. Although he was now a mature male, he left her with the same farewell he had used in his younger years. He gave her a playful look and slapped some leaves against her back.

As the holidays came near, Fossey experienced a growing sense of concern for the gorillas' safety. During this season, poaching tended to increase. Although she and her staff had been effective in destroying traps and taking away poachers' weapons, they had limited resources. They were not able to patrol constantly.

Farewell to Digit

On January 1, 1978, one of Fossey's trackers, Nemeye, came back to camp, unable to locate Group 4. The next day, Fossey and her staff went to search the region. Researcher Ian Redmond found Digit's damaged body.

In typical gorilla behavior, as the adult male, he had fought off poachers and their hunting dogs while the rest of the family escaped. He suffered several spear wounds. His head and hands had been cut off. The porters brought him back to camp, and his body was buried near the campsite. Fossey made a simple sign with his name on it.

Fossey was heartbroken. She wrote: "There are times when one cannot accept facts for fear of shattering one's being . . . all of Digit's life, since my first meeting with him as a playful little ball of

⬆ On the left is Digit's burial site.

fluff ten years earlier, passed through my mind. From that moment on, I came to live within an insulated part of myself."[3]

Raising Awareness

Fossey wrote letters to people to request aid in protecting the gorillas. Fossey wrote to the president of Rwanda, asking him to ensure harsh punishment for poachers. She knew that the president would be open to this idea. After all, it was Digit's poster that had attracted foreign tourists.

Ian Redmond suggested that they use Digit's death to attract the attention of the world to the gorillas' struggle for survival. Digit's death was announced on one of America's evening news programs. With Redmond, Fossey set up the Digit Fund to raise money to fight poachers. The fund would also promote active conservation of the parkland. In addition, she hired armed guards to protect the staff and students at Karisoke.

Fossey wanted to train natives to take on anti-poaching activities. Based on her long experience with the park management, she felt that the park guards could not be trusted. They could be bribed by poachers. According to Fossey, one of the few officials who helped her was the chef (chief) des Brigades, Paulin Nkubili. He organized forces to catch and arrest suspected poachers.

Uncle Bert

Group 4 needed increased protection from groups of poachers. Fossey knew they had to leave the saddle region between the mountains in which they had been roaming. She and her staff planned to bring them back to Mount Visoke. In order to bring the group back, the scientists and camp staff had to herd the gorillas. It was not a pleasant experience. Herding the gorillas meant that the humans had to pretend to be invisible pursuers, chasing the animals. The animals screamed in fright as they were driven to a safer location.

In mid-July, Uncle Bert led Group 4 back to the saddle. The region seemed safer because of an increase in patrols. But it was not safe. A new method of destruction was introduced—on July 24, Uncle Bert was shot.

Uncle Bert's body was buried next to Digit's. Like Digit, he died protecting his family. Fossey later realized that the likely cause of Uncle Bert's death was that the poachers were trying to capture his son, Kweli. They may have intended to send Kweli to a foreign zoo. This thought brought back depressing memories of her experience with Coco and Pucker.

Time to Leave Once More

In 1977, Fossey thought she had tuberculosis, a disease that affects the lungs, and traveled to the

United States for treatment. She was told she did not have the disease but that she needed surgery to heal a broken rib. She was in very poor health. She limped from a badly healed broken leg. She also now had to use an oxygen tank, although she continued to smoke. She was just over fifty years old, but she seemed much older.

Fossey was also in a full-scale war with the poachers. Her research time was limited, because she felt the need for constant vigilance. Members of the scientific community felt she was being distracted from the more important aspects of her work. In addition, she was developing a negative reputation.

Fossey was seen as being not only protective of the gorillas but unfriendly toward outsiders. The Leakey Foundation wanted Fossey to return to the United States to write about her research. The foundation threatened to cut off funding for her to stay at Karisoke. It was time for a break.

In 1979, she was given the chance to teach at Cornell University. She stayed for three years, occasionally visiting Africa. She left Sandy Harcourt, one of her students, in charge of Karisoke. Fossey entered a period that gave her a rest from the intensity of her work. But she knew she would eventually return to Africa for good.

7

Transitions

From 1979 to 1980, the Digit Fund's work began to take hold. Funding for patrols improved the gorillas' safety. The Humane Society of America donated funding that properly equipped and clothed the staff. Almost four thousand traps were torn down during the first eighteen months of the fund's operation, at a cost of only six dollars per day to feed and pay salaries to each man.

Also in 1979, Nunkie's group was growing. As the size of Nunkie's group increased, the gorillas wandered farther away. However, after one of the infants' ankles was cut by a wire trap, the group returned to the safer environment of Mount Visoke.

On New Year's Day in 1980, while Fossey was visiting Karisoke, an infant was brought to her door. A poacher had tried to sell the baby gorilla to a French doctor. Luckily, the doctor turned her over to Fossey for healing and protection. The baby was named Bonne Année ("Good Year"). Fossey was eventually able to return Bonne Année to the wilderness where she belonged. This outcome was a great relief, considering her painful memories of the time when Coco and Pucker had been sent to a zoo.

Under Sandy Harcourt's leadership, Karisoke became more focused on research. Workers there mostly collected data on the gorillas. However, poaching increased, and the camp fell into disrepair. After finishing up her commitment to Cornell and completing her book, *Gorillas in the Mist*, Fossey returned to Karisoke permanently in 1983.

Back in the Wonderful Wilderness

When Fossey went back to Karisoke, she became more and more isolated from the world at large. She spent more time with gorillas than with people.

One of the things she had learned during her experience at Karisoke was that there were very few people who could live in the wild for long periods of time. Certain people, such as photographer Robert Campbell and researcher Ian Redmond, were able to adapt to wilderness living fairly easily. For her, of course, living in the wild was her preference.

However, as students came and went, Fossey learned that some of them could not adjust to the physical strain of living at high altitudes with only basic comforts, along with extended periods of isolation from the outside world. Like Fossey, her research students had to be uniquely passionate and committed to their work in order to live in the Virungas.

1983

Fossey was still concerned about poaching, which had continued in her absence. By the end of 1983, she and her staff had destroyed more than 1,500 snares. Many poachers were captured and arrested. Still, by the time Fossey published *Gorillas in the Mist*, she was very concerned about the 242 gorillas in the Virungas. She did not think that there was enough energy being put toward their future and the generations that could follow them.

Fossey also worried about the impact of the continuous flow of visitors. The increase in tourists eventually killed Nunkie. He died from a human disease that his body couldn't fight. In addition, certain gorillas were beginning to act oddly. Some wandered away from their groups. Fossey's anxiety increased, since she felt sure that they were reacting to the growing presence of human strangers.

1985: Murder and Mystery

In December 1985, someone cut the metal outside of Dian Fossey's cabin and murdered her with a panga—a machete. Although her cabin was wrecked, and her belongings were spread all over the bedroom, there was no apparent robbery. The murderer was unknown.

Nine months later, student Wayne McGuire, who had left Rwanda by then, was charged with the crime, along with five Rwandans. Even today, more than twenty years later, the murder remains a mystery. It is generally agreed that McGuire was innocent and that the Rwandans wanted to blame an outsider. It is also generally agreed that Fossey's death was the result of her conflicts with poachers, even if they were not directly responsible. She had many enemies in Rwanda who saw her as an intruder in their world.

Four days after the murder, Dian Fossey was buried near her cabin, next to her beloved Digit. These words were put on her tombstone:

Nyiramachabelli
Dian Fossey
1932–1985
No one loved gorillas more
Rest in peace, dear friend
Eternally protected
In this sacred ground
For you are home
Where you belong

Positive Outcomes

After Fossey's death, the Digit Fund became Dian Fossey Gorilla Fund International. Today the Fund is vibrant and active. In addition, the Parc National des Volcans region is now protected by Rwandan laws.

What can we learn from Fossey's experience—her life, her work, and her death? For one thing, there are different approaches that people take to conservation and to the preservation of habitats. In addition, there are cultural differences that must be overcome to arrive at common goals.

Conservation

Fossey drew a sharp distinction between two kinds of conservation efforts. The first she called "active conservation," meaning the enforcement of antipoaching laws and serious penalties for poaching-related activities, such as the sale of animal parts. The second she labeled "theoretical conservation"—encouraging tourism, promoting

The coffin of American zoologist Dian Fossey is lowered into the ground by friends and co-workers in Mount Visoke, Rwanda, January 3, 1986.

gorilla habituation to humans, and educating people to respect the gorillas and their habitat.[1]

At the time of Fossey's work, theoretical conservation was more attractive to the Rwandan government, because it drew tourists to the area and had an economic benefit to the region. She was impatient with this approach, because it did not address what she felt were the immediate survival needs of the gorillas.

However, in her later years, she came to another realization. In order to get the full support of the Rwandans in protecting the mountain gorillas' habitat, she would have to make natives aware of how conservation would benefit them. In a country with a dense population, many of whose people depended on farming to live, there was little interest in protecting another species. Natives needed to understand that the mountains in which the gorillas lived also benefited them. The mountains were a water source for the crops they depended on.

If Rwandans protected the mountains, they would be ensuring their own survival, as well as that of the mountain gorilla. It was Fossey's hope that Rwanda could act as a model for the neighboring countries of Zaire (now the Democratic Republic of Congo) and Uganda. These nations included the Virunga volcanic range as part of their land.

"NYIRAMACHABELLI"

DIAN FOSSEY

1932 — 1985

NO ONE LOVED GORILLAS MORE

REST IN PEACE, DEAR FRIEND

ETERNALLY PROTECTED

IN THIS SACRED GROUND

FOR YOU ARE HOME

WHERE YOU BELONG

Dian Fossey

Wowe Nyiramacyibili wakunze u Rwanda
Ukihobera ingagi izo zo mu Birunga
Karisoke iyi wahanze ikaba ikubikirive
Iti gira amahoro uwurukundo rudakangwa umuheto.
Imana iguhe iruhuko radashira.

Fossey who worked to protect the endangered mountain gorillas in the Virungas, was found murdered in her cabin on December 26, 1985.

⬆ Sigourney Weaver, star of "Gorillas in the Mist," and friend.

The Future

Fossey's book, *Gorillas in the Mist,* tracks the years from 1967 to 1983 that she spent researching the mountain gorillas living in the dormant Virunga volcanoes. In it, she shares her personal commitment to these creatures. She also provides a glimpse into the day-to-day work of a field researcher. Even though she was not a traditional scientist, her careful observations and hard work provide valuable lessons.

One of Fossey's key contributions to the field is that within a fairly short time, she was able to create habituated groups of gorillas. Her unending patience and willingness to experiment with her own behavior allowed her to discover the gorillas' comfort level. Their habituation allows for researchers to continue observing gorilla behavior at close range to this day. They can be watched and followed by researchers, because they allow a human presence in their midst.

8

What Does the Future Hold?

The mountain gorillas that researchers know of live in two national parks. One group lives on the dormant Virunga volcanoes that border the Democratic Republic of Congo (in the Virungas National Park), Rwanda (in the Volcanoes National Park), and Uganda (in the Mgahinga National Park). The other group lives in southwest Uganda (in the Bwindi-Impenetrable National Park). Dian Fossey's research included the mountain gorillas in the Congo for a short time. The major portion of her time was spent studying the mountain gorillas in the Volcanoes National Park in Rwanda.

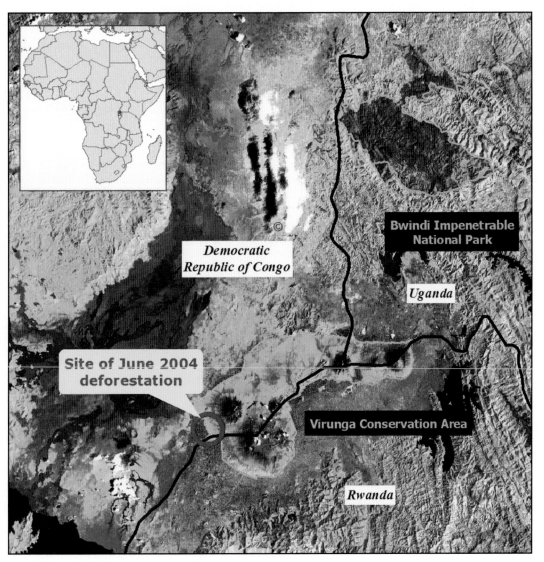

Democratic
Republic of Congo

Bwindi Impenetrable
National Park

Uganda

Site of June 2004
deforestation

Virunga Conservation Area

Rwanda

⬆ This NASA satellite image shows the Virunga volcanic range, home
to the mountain gorillas.

The number of mountain gorillas decreased during the 1970s and 1980s, and even into the early 1990s. Since that time, researchers have seen a 6% increase between 2002 and 2007 in Uganda's Impenetrable National Park, according to an online article from LiveScience on April 20, 2007, *Mountain Gorilla Population Rebounds in Uganda*.

Based on 2003 estimates, it appears that there are currently a total of about 720 mountain gorillas, according to the same article. In the Virunga volcanoes region, there are about 380 mountain gorillas, an increase of 17 percent over those counted in the Virungas in 1989. Of this group, around 70 percent are considered habituated to humans. This number is a huge percentage. Consider that when Fossey began her work in the 1960s, contact between mountain gorillas and humans had hardly begun!

The greatest increase in the mountain gorilla population has occurred in the Volcanoes National Park in Rwanda, where the Karisoke Research Center is located. There the animals are better protected and more often studied. In the Democratic Republic of Congo, the population has decreased. The mountain gorilla is considered endangered by the The International Union for the Conservation of Nature and Natural Resources (IUCN), also called the World Conservation Union.

Threats to Continued Survival

Specific threats to the mountain gorilla currently exist, despite the efforts of many people and organizations. These dangers include the small population of the mountain gorilla; the loss of its habitat; continued poaching; diseases from humans; and human conflicts.

Population Problems

The population of the mountain gorillas today is still very low, despite its increase since the time of Fossey's studies. Because their rate of reproduction is slow, the population has to be in the thousands to assure the future of the species. Like humans, mountain gorillas carry infants before birth for about nine months.

In addition, it takes a long period of time for males to reach maturity. Although they can reproduce from anywhere between the ages of nine and eleven, males do not usually mate at that time. After they develop their silver-colored backs between ages twelve and thirteen, they leave their original group to wander. It takes them a few years after that time to mate.

Habitat Loss

The mountain gorilla lives in a region where there are many humans who have always used the forest as a resource. Natives who keep cattle or plant

Deforestation remains a problem even in the protected park areas where mountain gorillas live. In this NASA image, the greener areas lie outside the boundaries of the Volcanoes National Park in Rwanda, while the brown areas with burning vegetation are inside Virunga National Park in the Congo.

crops destroy some of the gorillas' food sources. However, the needs of the natives must also be considered in developing a plan for the future. Conservationists agree that in order to protect the gorillas' habitat, they must work with the people who live in the region.

One problem is that forests are now also being destroyed by logging, creating deforestation. Wood is cut down either to sell or to use as fuel—thereby eliminating another source of food and living space.

The habitat of the mountain gorilla is already extremely limited. If the population continues to grow, even without outside threats, there will be a need to create new sustainable habitats for them.

In addition to needing their habitats protected, the mountain gorillas play a vital role in their habitats' survival. They take seeds and carry them from one area to another. This activity stimulates growth and encourages variation in the kinds of trees and vegetation in the forest. This variation helps maintain a healthy ecosystem.

Poaching

Although mountain gorillas are not often killed for their meat, they still are vulnerable to the traps set for other animals. In addition, infant gorillas are still sold illegally. And adult males are killed to capture the infants. As recently as 2007, the killing of ten mountain gorillas in the Democratic Republic of Congo was reported by the World Wildlife Fund.

Human Disease

Gorilla tourism has become popular for many reasons. It is a way for poorer nations to boost their economy. For visitors, it provides a way to learn about a species that is very close to our own. Visitors also enjoy the thrill of viewing an animal up close that was once thought to be dangerous.

However, tourism brings with it human diseases that gorillas are not equipped to fight off. The habituation of gorillas to humans has unfortunately become a problem. The gorillas are coming into increased contact with larger and larger human groups.

In Rwanda, there are strict controls placed on the number of tourists allowed to see the mountain gorillas. In addition, visiting hours are restricted. The posted rules of the Volcanoes National Park repeatedly warn visitors who feel unwell not to approach the mountain gorillas.

War

In Rwanda, the Volcanoes National Park was closed from 1991 to 1999 due to internal conflicts. Then the fighting in Rwanda expanded into the Democratic Republic of Congo. By 1994, more than eight hundred thousand refugees from Rwanda entered the mountain gorillas' forest habitats.

The refugees interrupted the lives of mountain gorillas in several ways. They took wood for fires and poached for animals. In addition, their presence disrupted the natural travel patterns of the gorillas. When the refugees left the area in 1996, additional conflict led to destruction of the Virungas National Park's resources. The political instability in the region has led to ongoing military activity, which further endangers the gorillas.

Protective Measures

In the Democratic Republic of Congo, Rwanda, and Uganda, there have been several laws passed to protect the present and future lives of the mountain gorillas. They prohibit the capture or hunting of mountain gorillas. However, it has been difficult for the three nations to enforce these laws, because there is little money to hire guards. In addition, the area in which the gorillas live has always been difficult to patrol.

All three parks are also listed as Natural World Heritage Sites. This status indicates that the protection of the mountain gorillas is an international priority. The mountain gorillas living in Volcanoes National Park in Rwanda also benefit from being near the Karisoke Research Center. Research is

A young female gorilla at a temporary shelter at the Dian Fossey Gorilla Fund International will be introduced back to the wild when she is able to socialize with other gorillas. She was taken from her family in the Virunga National Forest in Goma, Democratic Republic of the Congo.

continuing at Karisoke due to the efforts of the Dian Fossey Gorilla Fund International. Scientists there are actively engaged in studying the gorilla population and the effects of the outside world on it.

At Karisoke, trackers still destroy thousands of animal traps every year. They are well-trained and permitted to carry weapons. These patrollers work hard in an effort to stop the illegal killing and selling of animals for meat or other purposes.

The Dian Fossey Gorilla Fund International has also made progress in other areas. For example, the organization helps develop the economy of African communities. In addition, it uses Geographic Information Systems (GIS) technology to map the region, allowing students and trackers to become more familiar with the area. Another of the fund's tasks is to increase public awareness and education.

Time to Explore

You have read a great deal at this point about Dian Fossey and about mountain gorillas. What do you find most fascinating about Fossey and her work? What questions do you have about her work or its impact on mountain gorillas today? Does her work sound appealing or challenging? Think about aspects of her work that you would like to research, analyze, or discuss.

This mountain gorilla might not be alive today if Dian Fossey had not made the world aware of the species' plight more than thirty years ago.

For Possible Research

Choose a topic for further exploration and conduct Internet research. Present your work to others as a summary, article, dramatic presentation, photo essay, or another form that seems appropriate. You may wish to review the status of mountain gorillas today. How many are left? What does their future look like?

You might also consider looking at the researchers who are currently studying mountain gorillas. How does their work compare to Dian Fossey's? Is it important to continue studying this species? Why or why not?

For Possible Analysis

You have learned quite a bit from reading this book. You can read Fossey's firsthand account of her work by reading *Gorillas in the Mist*.

Based on your reading, you will have a good basis from which to judge the accuracy of the film. Think about the similarities and differences between the real life of Dian Fossey and the film's treatment of her life and work. Which makes a stronger emotional impact? Are there parts of the film that should have been done differently? If you were making a film about the life and work of Dian Fossey, would you make different choices?

⬥ For Discussion

A larger question is suggested by Fossey's experience. What role do humans play in relation to nature? Humans are part of nature, but we also have an impact on the natural world. Originally, Dian Fossey went into the wild to conduct research. Then she became passionate about the gorillas' long-term survival. She became a caretaker and manager of the wilderness to protect another species.

Some people have suggested that humans have a unique responsibility for the care of the natural world, especially since we have often had a destructive impact. If we decide that we have an effect on the world, how do we control our impact so that it is responsible and respectful?

Think about ways to define our role, and think about how you can use language to communicate what our role should be. Are we helpers? Protectors? Controllers? Which role do you think is appropriate?

You might wish to arrange a class debate on this question and have classmates take different positions. Or you may wish to conduct a group inquiry or survey to find out how others feel about this issue.

Dian Fossey's Life Highlights

1932—Dian Fossey is born in San Francisco, California.

1954—Fossey graduates from San Jose State College in California with a B.A. in occupational therapy

1963—Fossey travels to Africa and meets Louis Leakey. She sees mountain gorillas for the first time.

1966—Fossey returns to Africa to begin her study of mountain gorillas.

1967—Fossey sets up camp in Kabara but then is forced out of the Congo; she establishes a new camp at Karisoke Research Centre, Rwanda.

1969—Coco and Pucker are healed at Karisoke.

1970—Fossey was the first person to have voluntary contact with a gorilla, when Peanuts touched her hand. Fossey and her work are featured in *National Geographic* magazine.

1976—Fossey earns her doctorate at Cambridge University, Cambridge, England.

1977—Fossey's favorite gorilla, Digit, is killed by poachers. In response to this, she starts a campaign against gorilla poaching.

1978—The Digit Fund is established (now known as the Dian Fossey Gorilla Fund International). Uncle Bert is killed.

1983—Fossey returns full-time to Karisoke; *Gorillas in the Mist* is published.

1985—Dian Fossey is murdered at Karasoke.

1988—Fossey's life and work are portrayed in a movie based on her book. Sigourney Weaver stars as Dian Fossey and later becomes the honorary chairperson of the Dian Fossey Gorilla Fund International.

Glossary

archaeologist—Scientist who studies remains of past human life and activities.

blackback—Non-mature male mountain gorilla.

captivity—The state of being kept confined or enclosed.

captor—Person who keeps others confined.

conservationist—Person who tries to save nature and natural resources.

cultivate—To prepare use for raising crops.

deforestation—The action or process of clearing forests.

dehydrated—Suffering from a lack of water.

descendant—Member of a younger generation.

doctorate—Highest degree of scholarship.

dominant—Strongest; most powerful or controlling.

dormant—Inactive; temporarily not active.

ecosystem—Organisms and their environment functioning as an ecological unit.

evolution—The historical development of a biological group.

fine motor skills—Small movements of the hands, fingers, wrist, feet, toes.

forage—To search for food.

genetic—Relating to the makeup of living things.

group—A mountain gorilla family that travels together.

habitat—The environment where a plant or animal normally lives and grows.

habituation—The state of becoming used to something.

herd—To move in a group.

instability—The quality of being likely to change.

occupational therapist—Someone who works to help others return to activities of daily life.

offspring—Children.

panga—Large tool used for brush-cutter and as a weapon.

poacher—Someone who takes or kills animals illegally.

preservation—The state of being safe from injury, harm, or destruction.

Primate

primates—An order of mammals characterized by hands with opposable thumbs and finger nails instead of claws, binocular vision, and large brains. Humans, apes, monkeys, and related animals such as lemurs and tarsiers are all primates.

prohibit—To forbid based on rules or laws.

refugee—Person who flees to a foreign country or power to escape danger.

reproduction—The process by which plants and animals create offspring.

saddle region—Valley; area surrounded by mountainous slopes.

silverback—Leader of a mountain gorilla group; named for silver hair on its back.

species—Group of individuals sharing certain traits and given a common scientific name.

status—Position or rank in relation to others.

subspecies—Category that ranks immediately below species.

sustainable—Relating to a method of using a resource so that it is not used up or permanently damaged.

tracker—Someone who follows the trail or trace of an animal.

tuberculosis—Disease that affects especially the lungs and that is marked by fever, cough, and difficulty in breathing.

vocalization—Sound; utterance.

wean—To accustom a young child or animal used to food other than mother's milk.

zoology—Area of biology concerned with the classification and properties of animals.

Chapter Notes

Chapter 1. Digit's World

1. Dian Fossey, *Gorillas in the Mist* (Boston: Houghton Mifflin, 1983), p. 83.

Chapter 2. Dian Fossey's Early Life and the Beginning of Her Dream

1. Dian Fossey, *Gorillas in the Mist* (Boston: Houghton Mifflin, 1983), p. 4.

2. Farley Mowat, *Woman in the Mists: The Story of Dian Fossey and the Mountain Gorillas of Africa* (New York: Warner Books, Inc., 1987), p. 28.

Chapter 3. Adventures in Africa

1. Dian Fossey, *Gorillas in the Mist* (Boston: Houghton Mifflin, 1983), p. 55.

2. Ibid., p. 12.

3. Ibid., p. 157.

Chapter 4. Fieldwork Becomes Scholarship

1. Dian Fossey, *Gorillas in the Mist* (Boston: Houghton Mifflin, 1983), p. 48.

2. Ibid., p.11.

3. Ibid., p. 51.

4. Ibid., p. 141.

5. Ibid., p. 105.

6. Ibid., p. 175.

Chapter 5. Changes at Karisoke

1. Dian Fossey, *Gorillas in the Mist* (Boston: Houghton Mifflin, 1983), p. 91.

2. Farley Mowat, *Woman in the Mists: The Story of Dian Fossey and the Mountain Gorillas of Africa* (New York: Warner Books, Inc., 1987), p. 134.

3. Fossey, p. 155.

Chapter 6. Conflict
1. Dian Fossey, *Gorillas in the Mist* (Boston: Houghton Mifflin, 1983), p. 26.

2. Ibid., p. 122.

3. Ibid., p. 206.

Chapter 7. Transitions
1. Dian Fossey, *Gorillas in the Mist* (Boston: Houghton Mifflin, 1983), p. 58.

Further Reading

Bowman-Kruhm, Mary. *The Leakeys: A Biography.* Westport, Conn.: Greenwood Press, 2005.

de la Bédoyère, Camilla. *No One Loved Gorillas More: Dian Fossey, Letters From the Mist.* Washington, D.C.: National Geographic Society, 2005.

Fossey, Dian. *Gorillas In The Mist.* Boston: Houghton Mifflin, 1983, 2000.

Gilders, Michelle A. *The Nature Of The Great Apes: Our Next Of Kin.* Vancouver: Greystone Books, 2000.

Mara, Wil. *Dian Fossey: Among The Gorillas.* New York: Franklin Watts, 2004.

Matthews, Tom L., *Light Shining Through The Mist: A Photobiography of Dian Fossey*. Washington, D.C.: National Geographic Society, 1998.

Internet Sites

African Wildlife Foundation
<http://www.awf.org/content/wildlife/detail/mountaingorilla>

Dian Fossey Gorilla Fund International
<http://www.gorillafund.org>

***National Geographic:* Making Friends With Mountain Gorillas**
<ngm.nationalgeographic.com/2008/07/archive/fossey-gorillas-1970/dian-fossey-text

Index